Sacred Ties: Wedding Ceremonies through Anthropological Lens

Copyright Page

TITLE: Sacred Ties: Wedding Ceremonies through Anthropological Lens

1ST Edition

Copyright @ 2023

Roberto M. Rodriguez. All rights reserved.

ISBN: 9798223144885

Table of Contents

Sacred Ties: Wedding Ceremonies through Anthropological Lens

By Roberto Miguel Rodriguez

Chapter 1: Introduction

Background and Significance of Traditional Hindu Wedding Ceremonies

Introduction:

In this subchapter, we delve into the rich tapestry of Traditional Hindu Wedding Ceremonies, exploring their historical background, cultural significance, and the rituals that make them distinctive. As anthropologists, it is essential to understand the nuances of these ceremonies within the broader context of wedding rituals across different cultures and time periods. By doing so, we can gain insights into the interplay between tradition, religion, and social dynamics, shedding light on the unique aspects of Traditional Hindu Wedding Ceremonies.

Historical Background:

Traditional Hindu Wedding Ceremonies have a deep-rooted history that dates back thousands of years. The ancient Hindu texts, such as the Vedas and the Manusmriti, provide valuable insights into the origins and evolution of these ceremonies. Over time, these rituals have been shaped by regional variations, caste traditions, and cultural influences, resulting in a diverse array of wedding customs within the Hindu community.

Cultural Significance:

Hindu wedding ceremonies are not merely a union between two individuals but a union of two families, communities, and even deities. These ceremonies are steeped in symbolism and spirituality, with each ritual representing various aspects of married life and the couple's journey together. From the exchange of garlands symbolizing acceptance and love to the sacred fire that represents purity and transformation, each ritual holds profound significance in Hindu culture.

Unique Rituals:

One of the most striking aspects of Traditional Hindu Wedding Ceremonies is the sheer number of rituals involved. From the pre-wedding ceremonies like Mehendi and Haldi to the main wedding ceremony known as the Vivaah Sanskar, each ritual has its own symbolism and purpose. The sacred thread tying ceremony known as the Mangalsutra, the seven vows taken around the holy fire known as the Saptapadi, and the playful games like the stealing of the groom's shoes all contribute to the rich tapestry of Hindu wedding rituals.

Cross-Cultural Connections:

Traditional Hindu Wedding Ceremonies share commonalities with other indigenous, Buddhist, and Native American wedding ceremonies, emphasizing the universality of certain marriage rituals. Exploring these connections allows us to understand the cross-cultural influences and the ways in which cultural practices evolve and adapt over time.

Conclusion:

Traditional Hindu Wedding Ceremonies are a fascinating subject of study for anthropologists. By examining the historical background, cultural significance, and unique rituals associated with these ceremonies, we gain a deeper understanding of the intricate social fabric of Hindu society. Furthermore, exploring the connections between Traditional Hindu Wedding Ceremonies and other cultural and religious wedding traditions broadens our appreciation for the diversity and richness of human rituals across the globe.

Chapter 2: Traditional Hindu Wedding Ceremonies

The Concept of Marriage in Hinduism

Marriage is an integral part of Hindu society, and it holds immense significance in the lives of individuals and the community as a whole. In Hinduism, marriage is not merely a union between two individuals but a sacred bond that unites two families and ensures the continuity of lineage. This subchapter will delve into the profound concept of marriage in Hinduism, discussing its various aspects and the cultural significance it holds.

In Hinduism, marriage is seen as a sacrament, a divine institution that is meant to be cherished and respected. It is believed that marriage is a spiritual journey that enables individuals to fulfill their dharma (duty) and attain moksha (liberation). The union of two souls in marriage is seen as a union of two families, bringing together their values, traditions, and aspirations.

Traditional Hindu wedding ceremonies are elaborate affairs, consisting of numerous rituals and customs that symbolize various aspects of married life. From the auspicious moment of the couple's first meeting to the final ritual of the seven vows, each ceremony has a deep-rooted meaning and significance. These rituals encompass elements such as the exchange of garlands (varmala), the tying of the sacred thread (mangalsutra), and the circling of the sacred fire (saptapadi).

While Hindu wedding ceremonies have evolved over time, they have managed to retain their core essence and cultural heritage. In recent years, there has been an increasing interest in indigenous wedding ceremonies, as they provide a unique insight into the cultural practices and beliefs of different communities. Anthropologists have studied these ceremonies to understand the intricate interplay between culture, religion, and social dynamics.

Moreover, this subchapter will also explore the concept of marriage in relation to other niches, such as Buddhist wedding ceremonies, same-sex marriage ceremonies, destination wedding ceremonies, interfaith wedding ceremonies, African wedding ceremonies, Native American wedding ceremonies, medieval wedding ceremonies, and eco-friendly wedding ceremonies. By examining these diverse wedding traditions, anthropologists can gain a deeper understanding of the cultural diversity and complexities of marriage rituals worldwide.

In conclusion, the concept of marriage in Hinduism is a multifaceted phenomenon that encompasses spiritual, social, and cultural dimensions. By exploring traditional Hindu wedding ceremonies through an anthropological lens, researchers can uncover the intricate rituals and meanings associated with marriage in Hindu society. Additionally, by studying other wedding ceremonies, anthropologists can gain a broader perspective on the diversity of wedding rituals across different cultures and communities.

Pre-Wedding Rituals

In the realm of traditional Hindu wedding ceremonies, the importance of pre-wedding rituals cannot be overstated. These rituals hold deep cultural and religious significance, serving as a bridge between the past and the future, and symbolizing the union of two individuals and their families. As anthropologists delving into the intricate tapestry of wedding ceremonies, it is essential to understand the rich diversity and unique customs surrounding these pre-wedding rituals.

Pre-wedding rituals encompass a wide range of practices, each with its own purpose and symbolism. One such ritual is the Mehendi ceremony, where intricate henna designs are applied to the bride's hands and feet.

This ritual not only enhances the bride's beauty but also signifies love, happiness, and the strengthening of marital bonds. As anthropologists, we should explore the cultural nuances behind the patterns and motifs chosen, as they often reflect the bride's desires and her relationship with her future spouse.

Another significant pre-wedding ritual is the Haldi ceremony, where turmeric paste is applied to the bride and groom's bodies. This ritual is believed to purify and cleanse the couple, preparing them for their sacred union. It also serves as a moment of joyous celebration, with family and friends coming together to bless the couple and wish them a prosperous future. Studying the variations of this ritual across different regions and communities can shed light on the unique cultural practices and beliefs associated with it.

Furthermore, pre-wedding rituals in indigenous, Buddhist, and same-sex marriage ceremonies also offer fascinating insights into the diverse world of wedding traditions. Whether it is the exchange of symbolic gifts, sacred chants, or the performance of traditional dances, these rituals reflect the values and customs of the respective communities. By examining these rituals through an anthropological lens, we can better understand the intricate interplay between culture, religion, and personal beliefs in shaping these ceremonies.

Moreover, exploring pre-wedding rituals in destination, interfaith, African, Native American, medieval, and eco-friendly wedding ceremonies can provide valuable insights into the ways in which these ceremonies adapt and evolve over time. These rituals often blend ancient traditions with contemporary practices, highlighting the dynamic nature of wedding ceremonies and their ability to embrace change while preserving cultural heritage.

In conclusion, the subchapter on "Pre-Wedding Rituals" in "Sacred Ties: Exploring Traditional Hindu Wedding Ceremonies through

Anthropological Lens" offers a comprehensive exploration of the diverse pre-wedding rituals found in various wedding ceremonies. By delving into the cultural, religious, and social aspects of these rituals, anthropologists can gain a deeper understanding of the significance and symbolism embedded in these ceremonies. It is through this lens that we can truly appreciate the richness and complexity of wedding traditions across different cultures and communities.

Engagement Ceremony

In the world of Traditional Hindu Wedding Ceremonies, the Engagement Ceremony holds great significance as it marks the formal announcement of a couple's intention to marry. This subchapter will explore the intricacies of this enchanting event, shedding light on its cultural and anthropological significance.

The Engagement Ceremony, also known as Nishchitartham or Mangni, is a joyous occasion filled with traditions and rituals that vary across different regions of India. Anthropologists studying Indigenous Wedding Ceremonies will find the Engagement Ceremony in Hindu weddings particularly intriguing due to its ancient roots and the preservation of cultural practices.

Buddhist Wedding Ceremonies, on the other hand, may draw parallels to the Engagement Ceremony as both emphasize the importance of commitment and the union of two souls. This exploration will shed light on the similarities and differences between these two traditions.

Similarly, Same-Sex Marriage Ceremonies and Interfaith Wedding Ceremonies can benefit from understanding the Engagement Ceremony as it offers insights into the rituals and customs that bind couples together. This subchapter will explore how these modern ceremonies can adapt traditional practices to reflect the diversity and uniqueness of each couple.

For those interested in Destination Wedding Ceremonies, the Engagement Ceremony can serve as a starting point to understand how cultures intertwine when couples choose to celebrate their love in a foreign land. Additionally, African Wedding Ceremonies and Native American Wedding Ceremonies can draw inspiration from the Engagement Ceremony's symbolism of unity and commitment.

Delving into the world of Medieval Wedding Ceremonies, this subchapter will explore how the Engagement Ceremony has evolved over time and how it continues to hold its significance in modern times. The exploration will also touch upon the influence of Eco-friendly Wedding Ceremonies, emphasizing the importance of sustainability and ethical practices in the context of engagements.

By scrutinizing the Engagement Ceremony through an anthropological lens, this subchapter will provide valuable insights into the cultural, historical, and social aspects of Traditional Hindu Wedding Ceremonies. Readers from various niches will gain a deeper understanding of the diverse wedding traditions around the world and how they continue to shape the institution of marriage in contemporary society.

Mehndi Ceremony

The Mehndi ceremony is a vibrant and significant pre-wedding ritual in traditional Hindu wedding ceremonies. This subchapter explores the captivating world of Mehndi, delving into its historical background, cultural significance, and contemporary practices. Drawing upon anthropological research and fieldwork, this chapter offers a comprehensive understanding of this unique indigenous wedding ceremony.

Originating in ancient India, Mehndi holds a special place in Hindu wedding traditions. Derived from the Sanskrit word 'Mendhika,' meaning henna, Mehndi involves the application of intricate henna designs on the hands and feet of the bride-to-be. This ceremonial art form has deep-rooted cultural and religious significance, symbolizing love, beauty, and auspiciousness.

Anthropologists studying traditional Hindu wedding ceremonies will find the Mehndi ceremony particularly fascinating. The ritual serves as a platform for social interaction and community bonding, as family and friends gather to celebrate and participate in the joyous occasion. Observing and analyzing the intricate patterns and motifs of the Mehndi designs can provide valuable insights into the cultural and regional variations within the Hindu community.

Moreover, this subchapter explores the modern adaptations of the Mehndi ceremony, encompassing various niches of wedding ceremonies. From Buddhist wedding ceremonies to same-sex marriage ceremonies, the incorporation of the Mehndi ritual has transcended boundaries to foster inclusivity and diversity. Anthropologists studying interfaith wedding ceremonies, for instance, can examine how the Mehndi ceremony acts as a bridge between different religious and cultural traditions, symbolizing the union of families and communities.

Destination wedding ceremonies and eco-friendly wedding ceremonies also find inspiration in the Mehndi ceremony. As couples increasingly seek unique and sustainable wedding experiences, the Mehndi ritual offers an opportunity to embrace local customs and crafts. Anthropologists can explore how the Mehndi ceremony is adapted to different cultural contexts while preserving its essence and symbolic significance.

This subchapter also highlights the cross-cultural connections between Mehndi and other indigenous wedding ceremonies. From African to Native American wedding ceremonies, the art of adorning the body with natural pigments resonates across cultures, reflecting the universality of human expression and celebration.

By examining the Mehndi ceremony through an anthropological lens, this subchapter sheds light on the intricate tapestry of traditional Hindu wedding ceremonies and their intersections with diverse cultural practices. Through meticulous research and ethnographic studies, anthropologists can uncover the rich symbolism, social dynamics, and evolving meanings of this mesmerizing pre-wedding ritual.

Sangeet Ceremony

The Sangeet ceremony is a vibrant and joyous pre-wedding ritual that is an integral part of Traditional Hindu Wedding Ceremonies. In the book "Sacred Ties: Exploring Traditional Hindu Wedding Ceremonies through Anthropological Lens," we delve into the significance and cultural nuances of this enchanting ceremony.

The Sangeet ceremony is a celebration of music and dance, where family members and friends come together to rejoice in the union of two souls. Rooted in ancient Hindu traditions, this ceremony has evolved over the centuries, reflecting the diverse cultural heritage of the Indian subcontinent.

Anthropologists studying Traditional Hindu Wedding Ceremonies will find the Sangeet ceremony particularly intriguing. It offers a unique opportunity to observe the interplay of music, dance, and social dynamics, as it brings together people from different generations and backgrounds. Through this ceremony, one can witness the blending of traditional and contemporary elements, revealing the ever-evolving nature of cultural practices.

Moreover, the Sangeet ceremony holds relevance beyond the realm of Hindu weddings. Researchers exploring Indigenous Wedding Ceremonies, Buddhist Wedding Ceremonies, Same-Sex Marriage

Ceremonies, and Interfaith Wedding Ceremonies will find parallels and variations in the Sangeet ceremony across different cultures and faiths. It serves as a testament to the universality of music and dance as a means of celebration and bonding.

The Sangeet ceremony has also found its place in the modern world, with Destination Wedding Ceremonies gaining popularity. Couples and their families often choose exotic locations to host their Sangeet, creating a truly memorable experience for their guests. This subchapter will explore the unique elements of Sangeet ceremonies in these destination settings and the influence of the local culture on the celebration.

Additionally, the book "Sacred Ties" delves into the Sangeet ceremony in the context of African Wedding Ceremonies, Native American Wedding Ceremonies, Medieval Wedding Ceremonies, and Eco-friendly Wedding Ceremonies. By examining the Sangeet ceremony through an anthropological lens, we uncover the intricate connections between these diverse cultural practices, enriching our understanding of human traditions and rituals.

In conclusion, the Sangeet ceremony is a captivating aspect of Traditional Hindu Wedding Ceremonies, offering valuable insights to anthropologists studying various niches of wedding ceremonies. Through its exploration, we discover the universality of music and dance as a means of celebration, and the dynamic nature of cultural practices across different societies.

Wedding Rituals

Weddings are significant milestones in human life, representing the union of two individuals and the creation of a new family. Across cultures, wedding ceremonies are steeped in tradition and symbolism, reflecting the values, beliefs, and customs of the communities in which they take place. In the subchapter titled "Wedding Rituals" from the book "Sacred Ties: Exploring Traditional Hindu Wedding Ceremonies through Anthropological Lens," we delve into the fascinating world of various wedding rituals and their anthropological significance.

Traditional Hindu Wedding Ceremonies: Hindu weddings are rich in rituals, each with a specific purpose and meaning. From the colorful and joyous pre-wedding ceremonies to the sacred rituals performed during the wedding ceremony itself, this section explores the intricate details of Hindu wedding customs, such as the exchange of garlands, the sacred fire ceremony, and the seven steps taken around the fire.

Indigenous Wedding Ceremonies: Indigenous communities around the globe have diverse and unique wedding rituals that connect them to their ancestral roots. This section examines the wedding ceremonies of tribes like the Maasai people of Africa, the Navajo Native Americans, and the Aboriginal tribes of Australia, shedding light on their customs, symbolism, and the role of community in these sacred unions.

Buddhist Wedding Ceremonies: Buddhism, with its emphasis on mindfulness and compassion, brings a distinct flavor to wedding ceremonies. This section explores the simplicity and spiritual aspects of Buddhist weddings, including meditation, chanting, and the exchange of vows, as well as the role of monks or nuns in officiating these unions.

Same-Sex Marriage Ceremonies: In recent years, same-sex marriage ceremonies have gained recognition and acceptance worldwide. This section delves into the various rituals and customs that are adapted or created specifically for same-sex weddings, highlighting the significance of inclusivity and love in these ceremonies.

Destination Wedding Ceremonies: With the rise of travel and globalization, destination weddings have become popular among couples seeking unique experiences. This section examines the cultural implications and challenges of destination weddings, highlighting how couples navigate blending their own traditions with those of the location in which they choose to marry.

Interfaith Wedding Ceremonies: Interfaith marriages bring together individuals from different religious backgrounds, resulting in beautiful ceremonies that blend multiple traditions. This section explores the intricacies of interfaith weddings, including the negotiation of rituals, the inclusion of diverse religious symbols, and the importance of mutual respect and understanding.

African Wedding Ceremonies: Africa is a continent rich in cultural diversity, and its wedding ceremonies reflect this diversity. From the vibrant and lively celebrations of Nigerian weddings to the elaborate rites of passage in Ethiopian weddings, this section delves into the unique customs, rituals, and symbolism found across various African wedding traditions.

Native American Wedding Ceremonies: Native American wedding ceremonies are deeply rooted in spirituality and honor the connection between individuals, their ancestors, and the natural world. This section explores the rituals, dances, songs, and symbolic elements that make Native American weddings a profound and sacred experience.

Medieval Wedding Ceremonies: Traveling back in time, this section delves into the wedding rituals of the medieval era, exploring the customs and practices that characterized unions during this period. From arranged marriages to the role of the Catholic Church, this section uncovers the fascinating world of medieval wedding ceremonies.

Eco-friendly Wedding Ceremonies: With the growing concern for the environment, many couples are opting for eco-friendly wedding ceremonies. This section explores the various ways in which couples integrate sustainability into their weddings, from choosing eco-conscious venues and decor to incorporating environmentally friendly rituals and practices.

By examining these diverse wedding rituals through an anthropological lens, "Sacred Ties" offers a comprehensive understanding of the cultural, social, and symbolic dimensions of weddings across various communities. Whether you are an anthropologist exploring the intricacies of traditional Hindu wedding ceremonies or a curious reader interested in indigenous, interfaith, or eco-friendly wedding rituals, this subchapter provides a rich and insightful exploration of the diverse world of wedding ceremonies.

Ganesh Puja

Ganesh Puja: The Auspicious Beginnings of a Hindu Wedding Ceremony

In the vast tapestry of traditional Hindu wedding ceremonies, few events hold as much significance as the Ganesh Puja. This subchapter aims to explore the deep-rooted cultural and spiritual importance of this ritual, shedding light on the intricate customs and beliefs that shape the fabric of Hindu matrimonial practices. Anthropologists delving into the realm of Traditional Hindu Wedding Ceremonies, Indigenous Wedding Ceremonies, and Interfaith Wedding Ceremonies will find this exploration particularly insightful.

The Ganesh Puja, also known as Ganapati Puja, marks the auspicious beginning of a Hindu wedding. Ganesh, the elephant-headed deity, is revered as the remover of obstacles and the bestower of blessings. As such, invoking his presence is considered essential to ensure a smooth and harmonious union for the couple.

The ceremony typically takes place in the presence of the bride, groom, and their families. A priest leads the proceedings, guiding participants through a series of rituals. The centerpiece of the Puja is an intricately decorated idol or picture of Lord Ganesh, adorned with flowers and vibrant colors. The idol symbolizes the divine presence of Ganesh, and his blessings are sought to ensure a successful and obstacle-free wedding.

During the Puja, mantras are chanted, invoking the deity's blessings, while offerings of flowers, fruits, sweets, and incense are made. The priest leads the participants in these rituals, highlighting the significance of each action and its symbolic representation. The atmosphere is filled with devotion, as the families offer heartfelt prayers for a joyous and prosperous journey ahead.

Anthropologists exploring Indigenous Wedding Ceremonies and Native American Wedding Ceremonies will find parallels in the reverence for nature and the spiritual connection with the divine that permeate the Ganesh Puja. Similarly, those interested in Interfaith Wedding Ceremonies will discover the inclusive nature of Hindu rituals, as the Ganesh Puja welcomes people of all faiths to partake in its sacredness.

The Ganesh Puja transcends cultural boundaries and has also found its place in modern wedding trends. Destination Wedding Ceremonies are increasingly incorporating this ritual as a means to infuse traditional elements into exotic locales. Furthermore, Same-Sex Marriage Ceremonies have embraced the Ganesh Puja as a way to honor and celebrate love, irrespective of gender.

In conclusion, the Ganesh Puja is a cornerstone of Hindu wedding ceremonies, offering a glimpse into the rich tapestry of spiritual and cultural practices that shape these celebrations. Anthropologists studying Traditional Hindu Wedding Ceremonies, Indigenous Wedding Ceremonies, Interfaith Wedding Ceremonies, and other related niches will find this exploration invaluable in understanding the depth and significance of this sacred ritual.

Kanyadaan

Kanyadaan: The Sacrament of Giving Away the Bride

In the intricate tapestry of traditional Hindu wedding ceremonies, one of the most profound and emotionally charged rituals is the Kanyadaan. Derived from the Sanskrit words "kanya" meaning daughter and "daan" meaning donation, Kanyadaan symbolizes the act of giving away the bride by her parents with blessings and love.

For anthropologists studying Traditional Hindu Wedding Ceremonies, Kanyadaan offers a fascinating lens into the cultural significance of marriage and kinship. Rooted in ancient scriptures and customs, this ritual reflects the sacred bond between families and the transition of a daughter from her natal home to her marital home.

Kanyadaan rituals vary across diverse cultures and regions within the vast Hindu diaspora. From vibrant North Indian weddings to serene South Indian ceremonies, the essence remains the same – to honor the bride's parents as they entrust their daughter to her groom, symbolizing the union of two families.

This subchapter also appeals to anthropologists specializing in Indigenous Wedding Ceremonies, as Kanyadaan shares similarities with other indigenous cultures where the bride's family plays a crucial role in the wedding process. By delving into the nuances of Kanyadaan, researchers can draw parallels and uncover the universal themes of family, love, and community present in indigenous wedding ceremonies worldwide.

Furthermore, the subchapter explores how Kanyadaan adapts to modern societal changes. With the rise of same-sex marriage ceremonies, interfaith unions, and destination weddings, questions arise about how Kanyadaan can be reinterpreted to accommodate these evolving dynamics. The chapter examines how these alternative wedding ceremonies reimagine Kanyadaan, questioning and challenging traditional gender roles and family structures.

Additionally, the subchapter highlights the significance of Kanyadaan in the context of African, Native American, and medieval wedding ceremonies. By comparing and contrasting these diverse cultural practices, anthropologists gain valuable insights into the universality of the human experience and the ways in which marriage rituals reflect societal values and beliefs.

Lastly, the subchapter explores the growing trend of eco-friendly wedding ceremonies. As the world grapples with environmental challenges, couples are seeking ways to align their wedding rituals with sustainability. This chapter explores how Kanyadaan and other wedding ceremonies can be adapted to embrace eco-consciousness, incorporating elements of nature, reducing waste, and promoting ethical practices.

In conclusion, the subchapter on Kanyadaan in "Sacred Ties: Exploring Traditional Hindu Wedding Ceremonies through Anthropological Lens" provides anthropologists with a rich tapestry of cultural, historical, and contemporary insights. It invites them to explore the intricacies of Kanyadaan within the realms of Traditional Hindu Wedding Ceremonies, Indigenous Wedding Ceremonies, Buddhist Wedding Ceremonies, Same-Sex Marriage Ceremonies, Destination Wedding Ceremonies, Interfaith Wedding Ceremonies, African Wedding Ceremonies, Native American Wedding Ceremonies, Medieval Wedding Ceremonies, and Eco-friendly Wedding Ceremonies. By delving into this ancient ritual, anthropologists gain a deeper understanding of the profound cultural and social meanings embedded in the act of giving away the bride.

Phere

Phere: The Sacred Circumambulation in Hindu Wedding Ceremonies

In the realm of Traditional Hindu Wedding Ceremonies, one of the most significant rituals is the Phere. This subchapter delves into the intricacies of this ancient custom, exploring its symbolism, cultural significance, and anthropological insights. Anthropologists studying Indigenous Wedding Ceremonies, Buddhist Wedding Ceremonies, Same-Sex Marriage Ceremonies, Destination Wedding Ceremonies, Interfaith Wedding Ceremonies, African Wedding Ceremonies, Native American Wedding Ceremonies, Medieval Wedding Ceremonies, and Eco-friendly Wedding Ceremonies will find valuable insights within this chapter.

The Phere is a ritualistic circumambulation around the sacred fire, known as the Agni, by the bride and groom. It symbolizes their journey through the various stages of life, together as partners. This ritual marks the transition from individuality to the sacred union of marriage, where the couple becomes one entity. The Phere consists of seven rounds, each round symbolizing a specific vow and commitment made by the couple.

Anthropologists studying Traditional Hindu Wedding Ceremonies will find the Phere to be an intriguing practice. It reflects the deep-rooted cultural beliefs and values prevalent in Hindu society. The significance of fire in the ceremony represents purity, transformation, and the divine presence. Furthermore, the seven rounds symbolize the seven sacred rivers in Hindu mythology, emphasizing the importance of nature and the elements in Hindu rituals.

For those interested in Indigenous Wedding Ceremonies, the Phere offers insights into the similarities and differences between various cultural practices. While the specifics may differ, the underlying themes of unity, commitment, and the sacredness of marriage remain constant across indigenous cultures.

Additionally, the Phere holds relevance in the context of Same-Sex Marriage Ceremonies, where it can be adapted to honor the union of two individuals regardless of gender. This ritual can be reinterpreted to reflect the unique experiences and aspirations of same-sex couples, reinforcing the idea of love and commitment in diverse relationships.

Destination Wedding Ceremonies are becoming increasingly popular, and the Phere can serve as a captivating addition to such ceremonies. Incorporating this ritual into a destination wedding can provide a deeper cultural experience for the couple and their guests, fostering an appreciation for the rich heritage of Hindu traditions.

Interfaith Wedding Ceremonies also find inspiration in the Phere. As couples from different religious backgrounds come together, this ritual can serve as a unifying element, showcasing the willingness to embrace and respect each other's beliefs.

African Wedding Ceremonies, Native American Wedding Ceremonies, and Medieval Wedding Ceremonies can draw parallels to the Phere, exploring the role of fire and the symbolism of circumambulation in their respective rituals. These connections shed light on the shared human experiences and the ways in which different cultures express their sacred unions.

Lastly, for those studying Eco-friendly Wedding Ceremonies, the Phere offers an opportunity to explore the relationship between culture, tradition, and sustainable practices. Incorporating eco-friendly elements into the ritual can promote environmental consciousness, aligning ancient customs with modern concerns.

In conclusion, the Phere is a ritual that transcends cultural boundaries, offering anthropologists insights into not only Traditional Hindu Wedding Ceremonies but also a plethora of other cultural practices. Its symbolism, cultural significance, and adaptability make it a fascinating subject of study for those interested in exploring the diverse realms of wedding ceremonies.

Sindoor Daan

Sindoor Daan: The Sacred Ritual of Vermilion Application in Hindu Weddings

In the vast tapestry of Hindu wedding ceremonies, the ritual of Sindoor Daan holds a special place. This subchapter will explore the significance of Sindoor Daan, a ritualistic act that involves the application of vermillion on the bride's forehead, and its role in traditional Hindu wedding ceremonies.

The practice of Sindoor Daan can be traced back to ancient Hindu texts and is deeply rooted in symbolism and cultural beliefs. Considered a mark of a married woman in Hindu society, the application of sindoor is believed to bring good fortune, protect the husband's life, and ensure marital bliss. The sindoor, a red powder made from turmeric and lime, represents both the strength and the vulnerability of a woman.

Anthropologists studying Hindu wedding ceremonies will find Sindoor Daan to be a fascinating aspect of the rituals. It reflects the cultural values and gender dynamics prevalent in traditional Hindu society. The ritual emphasizes the importance of a woman's role as a wife and her commitment to her marital duties, while also symbolizing her status as a protector of her husband's well-being.

This subchapter will not only explore the ritual's significance but also delve into the diverse variations of Sindoor Daan across different regions and communities. From the elaborate application of sindoor on the bride's hair parting to the simpler dot on the forehead, the ways in which Sindoor Daan is performed can vary greatly. This variation allows for a deeper understanding of the cultural diversity within Hindu society.

Furthermore, this subchapter will also examine how Sindoor Daan has evolved over time to accommodate changing societal norms and values. With the rise of interfaith and same-sex marriages, the ritual has adapted to become more inclusive and reflective of the diverse range of individuals partaking in Hindu wedding ceremonies.

By studying the ritual of Sindoor Daan, anthropologists gain insights not only into Hindu wedding ceremonies but also into wider themes such as gender roles, cultural traditions, and the ways in which rituals adapt to changing social contexts. This subchapter will provide a comprehensive analysis of Sindoor Daan, catering to the interests of anthropologists specializing in traditional Hindu wedding ceremonies, indigenous wedding ceremonies, Buddhist wedding ceremonies, same-sex marriage ceremonies, destination wedding ceremonies, interfaith wedding ceremonies, African wedding ceremonies, Native American wedding ceremonies, medieval wedding ceremonies, and eco-friendly wedding ceremonies.

Post-Wedding Rituals

In the rich tapestry of traditional Hindu wedding ceremonies, the post-wedding rituals hold a special place. These rituals are not only a continuation of the sacred bond created during the wedding ceremony but also serve as a way to welcome the newlyweds into their new life together. Anthropologists studying traditional Hindu wedding ceremonies will find these post-wedding rituals fascinating, as they offer insights into the cultural and social fabric of Hindu society.

One of the most prominent post-wedding rituals is the Griha Pravesh, which translates to "entering the home." In this ritual, the bride is welcomed into her husband's home as a symbol of her new role as a wife and daughter-in-law. The ceremony involves the couple seeking blessings from the elders of the family and conducting various rituals to ensure prosperity and happiness in their new life.

Another intriguing post-wedding ritual is the Vidaai, which marks the departure of the bride from her parental home. This emotional ritual sees the bride bidding farewell to her family and friends, symbolizing her transition from her natal home to her marital home. The Vidaai is often accompanied by tearful goodbyes, joyful celebrations, and a sense of mixed emotions that anthropologists can explore to understand the dynamics of familial relationships and gender roles in Hindu society.

In addition to these rituals, there are several other post-wedding customs that vary across regions and communities within the vast landscape of Hinduism. These include the reception ceremony, where the couple is officially introduced to the extended family and friends, and the playful Rasam Pagri, where the groom's turban is playfully stolen by the bride's sisters and then returned in exchange for a small monetary gift.

Anthropologists specializing in indigenous, Buddhist, same-sex, destination, interfaith, African, Native American, medieval, and eco-friendly wedding ceremonies will also find value in studying these post-wedding rituals. By comparing and contrasting the post-wedding customs across various cultural and religious contexts, researchers can gain a deeper understanding of how marriage rituals reflect and shape societal norms, gender dynamics, and cultural identities.

The exploration of post-wedding rituals in traditional Hindu wedding ceremonies opens up a world of insights into the complexities of human relationships, cultural practices, and belief systems. It invites anthropologists to delve into the fascinating realm of wedding ceremonies and understand the significance of these rituals in shaping and preserving cultural heritage.

Griha Pravesh

Griha Pravesh: The Sacred Threshold

In the realm of Traditional Hindu Wedding Ceremonies, there exists a significant ritual known as Griha Pravesh, which translates to "Entering the House." This subchapter delves into the depths of this profound ceremony, exploring its cultural significance and anthropological implications.

Griha Pravesh marks the moment when the newlywed couple steps into their new abode, their marital home, for the very first time. It is a symbolic crossing of the threshold, representing the beginning of their journey as a married couple. This ritual holds immense importance in Hindu culture, as it signifies the establishment of a new household and the fusion of two families.

Anthropologists studying Indigenous Wedding Ceremonies will find Griha Pravesh particularly intriguing, as it provides a unique insight into the customs and practices of Hindu communities. The ceremony is deeply rooted in ancient traditions and often involves elaborate rituals and blessings from family elders. Through their research, anthropologists can uncover the social dynamics and kinship ties that shape these ceremonies, shedding light on the cultural fabric of Hindu society.

Moreover, Griha Pravesh holds relevance to researchers exploring Buddhist Wedding Ceremonies, as it shares some commonalities with Buddhist rituals. Both traditions emphasize the importance of harmony, auspiciousness, and the integration of spiritual beliefs into the marriage journey. By comparing and contrasting these ceremonies, anthropologists can deepen their understanding of the diverse practices within the broader umbrella of Indian weddings.

The subchapter also caters to a niche audience interested in Same-Sex Marriage Ceremonies, as it raises questions around the inclusion and adaptation of Griha Pravesh for such couples. Exploring how same-sex partners navigate this tradition can shed light on the evolving nature of wedding ceremonies and the negotiation of cultural norms in contemporary society.

Moreover, the subchapter touches upon Destination Wedding Ceremonies, Interfaith Wedding Ceremonies, African Wedding Ceremonies, Native American Wedding Ceremonies, Medieval Wedding Ceremonies, and Eco-friendly Wedding Ceremonies, outlining the potential intersections and adaptations of Griha Pravesh in these contexts.

In conclusion, Griha Pravesh serves as a pivotal moment in Traditional Hindu Wedding Ceremonies, offering anthropologists a rich field of study. By unpacking its symbolism, cultural nuances, and adaptations across various niches, researchers can gain valuable insights into the social, cultural, and historical aspects of marriage ceremonies, ultimately contributing to a deeper understanding of the human experience.

Reception Ceremony

The Reception Ceremony holds a significant place in the tapestry of Traditional Hindu Wedding Ceremonies. It is an event that brings together the families and friends of the bride and groom, allowing them to celebrate their union in a joyous and festive manner. As anthropologists, we have the privilege of exploring and understanding the intricacies of this ceremony and its cultural significance.

In Hindu culture, the Reception Ceremony is a grand affair that follows the solemnity of the wedding rituals. It is an opportunity for the newlyweds to be introduced to their extended families and friends, as well as for their families to showcase their happiness and blessings for the couple. The event is typically characterized by elaborate decorations, sumptuous feasts, and lively music and dance performances.

This subchapter delves into the various aspects of the Reception Ceremony, examining its unique elements across different cultures and contexts. We explore how Indigenous Wedding Ceremonies incorporate their traditional customs and rituals into the reception, creating a seamless blend of ancient traditions and modern celebrations. Buddhist Wedding Ceremonies, on the other hand, emphasize simplicity and mindfulness in their reception ceremonies, reflecting the core principles of their faith.

We also shed light on the evolving landscape of wedding ceremonies, such as Same-Sex Marriage Ceremonies. The Reception Ceremony becomes a platform for the LGBTQ+ community to celebrate their love and commitment in front of their loved ones, challenging societal norms and promoting inclusivity.

Furthermore, we explore Destination Wedding Ceremonies, where couples choose exotic locations as a backdrop to their reception. This trend has gained popularity in recent years, as couples seek unique and memorable experiences for themselves and their guests.

Interfaith Wedding Ceremonies present another fascinating aspect of the Reception Ceremony. These ceremonies showcase the harmonious blending of different religious and cultural traditions, celebrating the diversity and unity of love.

This subchapter also delves into African Wedding Ceremonies, Native American Wedding Ceremonies, and Medieval Wedding Ceremonies, highlighting their distinct reception customs and practices. From the vibrant colors and rhythmic dances of African weddings to the symbolic rituals of Native American ceremonies, we explore the rich cultural heritage embedded in these celebrations.

Lastly, we touch upon the growing trend of Eco-friendly Wedding Ceremonies. In an era of increasing environmental consciousness, couples are adopting sustainable practices in their reception ceremonies, from using biodegradable decorations to serving locally sourced, organic food.

Through this subchapter, we invite anthropologists to immerse themselves in the diverse world of Reception Ceremonies, understanding their cultural significance and exploring the ways in which they continue to evolve and adapt in different contexts. By studying these ceremonies through an anthropological lens, we gain valuable insights into the human experience, the celebration of love, and the preservation of cultural heritage.

Vidaai

Vidaai: The Bittersweet Farewell in Hindu Wedding Ceremonies

In the realm of Hindu wedding ceremonies, the Vidaai holds a significant place, encapsulating a myriad of emotions and cultural nuances. This subchapter explores the intricacies of this ritual, shedding light on its symbolism, evolution, and cultural variations within the diverse tapestry of traditional Hindu wedding ceremonies. Anthropologists studying the intricacies of indigenous, Buddhist, same-sex, destination, interfaith, African, Native American, medieval, and eco-friendly wedding ceremonies will find this exploration particularly enlightening.

Vidaai, also known as the bride's farewell, marks the poignant moment when the bride bids adieu to her natal home and embarks on a new journey with her husband. This ritual is characterized by a bittersweet amalgamation of emotions, as the bride's family experiences both joy for her new life and sorrow for her departure. The Vidaai serves as a powerful symbol of transition, reminding us of the transformative nature of marriage.

Within Hinduism, countless regional and cultural variations shape the Vidaai ceremony. From the tearful farewells in North Indian weddings to the playful and joyous send-offs in South Indian weddings, each region adds its unique flavor to this ritual. Anthropologists specializing in indigenous wedding ceremonies will find parallels between the Vidaai and similar farewell rituals in indigenous cultures, highlighting the universal significance of bidding adieu to one's ancestral home.

As the world embraces diverse forms of love and commitment, same-sex marriage ceremonies are gaining recognition and importance. In this context, the Vidaai ritual takes on a new meaning, transcending gender and emphasizing the emotional and psychological aspects of parting ways with one's family and embracing a new life partner.

Furthermore, the Vidaai is not confined to the boundaries of Hinduism alone. It finds echoes in other cultures and religions, such as the departure of the bride in African and Native American wedding ceremonies, or the farewell rituals in Buddhist wedding ceremonies. Even medieval wedding ceremonies, with their emphasis on social status and alliances, incorporated elements that echo the essence of the Vidaai.

In the modern era, destination weddings and interfaith marriages have become increasingly common. The Vidaai, in these contexts, becomes a bridge between cultures, as families from different backgrounds come together to bid farewell to the bride. Additionally, the rising importance of eco-friendly practices has influenced the Vidaai, with couples opting for sustainable materials and practices during this ritual.

The Vidaai, with its emotional depth and cultural significance, serves as a microcosm of the broader tapestry of traditional Hindu wedding ceremonies. Anthropologists delving into the intricacies of wedding rituals will find this subchapter a valuable resource, providing insights into the Vidaai's symbolism, regional variations, and its relevance in a diverse range of wedding ceremonies worldwide.

Chapter 3: Indigenous Wedding Ceremonies

Overview of Indigenous Wedding Traditions

Indigenous wedding traditions hold a profound significance in the fabric of cultural heritage around the world. These sacred ceremonies reflect the deep-rooted traditions and values of indigenous communities, fostering a sense of communal belonging and preserving their ancestral customs. In this subchapter, we will delve into the enchanting world of indigenous wedding traditions, with a focus on the captivating rituals and beliefs practiced in various indigenous cultures.

Traditional Hindu Wedding Ceremonies: Hindu weddings are known for their elaborate rituals and vibrant celebrations. We will explore the intricate customs such as the Mehendi ceremony, Saptapadi, and Kanyadaan, which symbolize the union of two souls and families.

Buddhist Wedding Ceremonies: Buddhist wedding ceremonies are rooted in simplicity and mindfulness. We will examine rituals such as the exchange of vows, offering of blessings, and the significance of the wedding mandala, which symbolizes the interconnectedness of all beings.

Same-Sex Marriage Ceremonies: In recent years, same-sex marriage ceremonies have gained recognition and acceptance worldwide. We will explore diverse indigenous cultures, such as the Native American Two-Spirit tradition and the Hijra community in India, which have long embraced and celebrated same-sex unions.

Destination Wedding Ceremonies: With the rise of destination weddings, many couples choose to celebrate their love in breathtaking locations. We will discuss indigenous wedding traditions in popular destinations like Mexico, Hawaii, and Bali, and their incorporation into these modern wedding settings.

Interfaith Wedding Ceremonies: Interfaith weddings bring together individuals from different religious backgrounds, creating a beautiful tapestry of traditions. We will explore how indigenous cultures navigate interfaith unions, respecting and honoring the beliefs of both partners.

African Wedding Ceremonies: The richness and diversity of African wedding traditions are awe-inspiring. From the jumping of the broom in African American weddings to the vibrant attire and ceremonial dances in weddings across the continent, we will explore the unique customs that make these celebrations truly unforgettable.

Native American Wedding Ceremonies: Native American wedding ceremonies vary across tribes, each with its distinct rituals and symbolism. We will delve into the sacred traditions of tribes like the Navajo, Apache, and Cherokee, exploring their connection to nature, spirits, and ancestral lineage.

Medieval Wedding Ceremonies: Travel back in time to the medieval era, where weddings were steeped in tradition and symbolism. We will uncover the fascinating customs of medieval Europe, including the exchange of rings, the crowning ceremony, and the significance of the wedding feast.

Eco-friendly Wedding Ceremonies: In an era of increasing environmental consciousness, eco-friendly wedding ceremonies have gained popularity. We will explore indigenous cultures that have long practiced sustainable wedding traditions, incorporating natural elements, and promoting environmental stewardship.

Join us on this captivating journey as we explore the world of indigenous wedding traditions, immersing ourselves in the beauty, diversity, and cultural significance of these sacred ceremonies. Through an anthropological lens, we will gain a deeper understanding of the intricate customs and beliefs that bind communities together and celebrate love in its myriad forms.

Native American Wedding Ceremonies

Native American wedding ceremonies are rich in cultural traditions and symbolism. These ceremonies vary greatly among different tribes, reflecting the diversity and uniqueness of Native American cultures. This subchapter will explore the fascinating world of Native American wedding rituals, shedding light on their significance and the anthropological insights they offer.

Native American wedding ceremonies are deeply rooted in spirituality and respect for nature. They often take place outdoors, in settings that hold spiritual significance to the tribe. Nature is considered an integral part of the ceremony, with the belief that the natural world is interconnected with human existence.

One common element in Native American wedding ceremonies is the exchange of vows. These vows are not only promises made between the couple but also commitments made to the community and the spiritual world. The couple may express their intentions to live harmoniously, to honor their ancestors, and to contribute positively to their tribe.

Another important aspect of Native American wedding ceremonies is the use of traditional attire and adornments. The couple may wear intricately designed garments, representing their tribal heritage and personal identity. Jewelry, feathers, and other accessories are also used to symbolize spiritual connections and blessings.

Rituals involving the elements of earth, fire, water, and air are often incorporated into Native American wedding ceremonies. These rituals serve to purify and bless the couple, as well as to invoke the presence of ancestral spirits. The use of sacred herbs, such as sage or sweetgrass, is common in these rituals.

Music and dance play a vital role in Native American wedding ceremonies. Traditional songs and dances are performed to celebrate the union of the couple and to invoke blessings from the spiritual realm. These performances are not only a form of entertainment but also a means of spiritual expression and communication.

By studying Native American wedding ceremonies, anthropologists gain valuable insights into the cultural beliefs, social structures, and spiritual practices of these indigenous communities. These ceremonies provide a window into the rich tapestry of Native American cultures and their deep connection to the natural world.

Understanding Native American wedding ceremonies also fosters appreciation for the diversity of wedding rituals across different cultures. It highlights the importance of cultural preservation and respect for traditions, as well as the potential for cross-cultural exchange and adaptation in contemporary wedding practices.

In conclusion, Native American wedding ceremonies offer anthropologists a unique lens through which to explore the intricate connections between culture, spirituality, and nature. By delving into the symbolism and rituals of these ceremonies, anthropologists can uncover valuable insights into the traditions and beliefs of Native American communities, while also gaining a deeper understanding of the broader spectrum of wedding ceremonies worldwide.

African Wedding Ceremonies

In this subchapter, we will delve into the rich and diverse tapestry of African wedding ceremonies. Africa is a continent renowned for its cultural diversity, with each region and ethnic group having distinct traditions and customs when it comes to marriage celebrations. As anthropologists, it is essential that we explore and understand these unique practices to gain insights into the social, cultural, and historical aspects of African societies.

African wedding ceremonies are vibrant, joyous, and deeply rooted in tradition. They often serve as a reflection of the community's values and beliefs, encompassing rituals that have been passed down through generations. These ceremonies are not merely events for the couple but involve the entire community, as marriage is seen as a union between families rather than just individuals.

One fascinating aspect of African wedding ceremonies is the use of vibrant colors and elaborate attire. Traditional African clothing, such as the iconic Kente cloth in West Africa or the Maasai attire in East Africa, plays a significant role in these celebrations. The colors and patterns of the garments often symbolize concepts like fertility, prosperity, and unity.

Rituals and customs vary across different African cultures. For instance, in Yoruba weddings in Nigeria, the couple undergoes a series of rituals, including the exchange of gifts and the tying of the bride's waist with a gele (headscarf) to symbolize her commitment to her husband. In contrast, in Zulu weddings in South Africa, the bride's family presents the groom with a list of items he must provide to prove his ability to care for their daughter.

Traditional African wedding ceremonies often involve music, dance, and storytelling, adding an element of celebration and communal bonding. Drumming, singing, and traditional instruments, such as the djembe or mbira, create a lively and uplifting atmosphere. Additionally, the presence of elders and spiritual leaders is crucial, as they bless the union and offer guidance to the couple.

It is important to note that African wedding ceremonies are not static, but rather dynamic and adaptive to changing times. In recent years, many couples have incorporated elements of modernity into their ceremonies, such as Western-style wedding gowns or exchanging rings. This blending of traditions reflects the evolving nature of African societies and the influence of globalization.

By studying African wedding ceremonies, anthropologists gain valuable insights into the social fabric, cultural heritage, and identity of African communities. Furthermore, understanding the diversity and complexities of these ceremonies allows us to appreciate the significance of marriage as a universal human experience while respecting the uniqueness of each culture's practices.

Chapter 4: Buddhist Wedding Ceremonies

Introduction to Buddhist Wedding Traditions

Buddhist wedding traditions offer a unique insight into the spiritual and cultural practices of this ancient religion. From the rich symbolism to the emphasis on mindfulness and compassion, these ceremonies are a beautiful blend of tradition and spirituality. In this chapter, we will explore the key elements of Buddhist wedding traditions, shedding light on their significance and how they have evolved over time.

Buddhist wedding ceremonies are deeply rooted in the teachings of Gautama Buddha, the founder of Buddhism. They emphasize the importance of harmony, respect, and commitment within a relationship. Unlike many other wedding ceremonies, Buddhist weddings are often simple and intimate, focusing on the union of two individuals rather than extravagant displays of wealth.

One of the central aspects of a Buddhist wedding is the exchange of vows. These vows typically include a commitment to support each other on the path of enlightenment, to practice loving-kindness and compassion, and to cultivate a harmonious and peaceful relationship. The vows reflect the Buddhist belief in the interconnectedness of all beings and the importance of nurturing a relationship that benefits not only the couple but also the wider community.

Another integral part of a Buddhist wedding is the chanting of sacred texts and prayers. These chants serve to bless and purify the couple, their families, and the entire ceremony. They also remind everyone present of the impermanence of life and the need to cultivate mindfulness in their relationships.

In Buddhist wedding ceremonies, the exchange of rings holds great significance. The wedding rings symbolize the eternal nature of love and the interconnectedness of all beings. The act of exchanging rings is a powerful reminder of the commitment the couple is making to each other and to their shared spiritual journey.

Throughout the ceremony, the presence of Buddhist monks or nuns is common. These spiritual leaders guide the couple and their families through the rituals, offering blessings and teachings that encourage a deep understanding of the Buddhist principles that underpin the marriage.

By exploring Buddhist wedding traditions, we gain a deeper understanding of the values and beliefs that shape these ceremonies. We can appreciate the simplicity and mindfulness that define these rituals and their focus on fostering compassion, harmony, and spiritual growth within a relationship. Whether you are an anthropologist studying traditional Hindu wedding ceremonies, indigenous wedding ceremonies, or any other niche within the realm of wedding traditions, understanding Buddhist wedding traditions will provide valuable insights into the diversity and complexity of human culture and rituals.

Rituals and Symbolism in Buddhist Weddings

Buddhist weddings, like many other traditional wedding ceremonies, are steeped in rituals and symbolism that hold deep spiritual and cultural significance. These ceremonies reflect the teachings and principles of Buddhism, emphasizing mindfulness, compassion, and the interconnectedness of all beings. In this subchapter, we will explore the various rituals and symbolism unique to Buddhist weddings, shedding light on the rich tapestry of traditions that exist within this ancient religion.

One of the most prominent rituals in a Buddhist wedding is the exchange of vows. Unlike Western weddings, where couples often recite personalized vows, Buddhist weddings follow a more traditional script that emphasizes the values of Buddhism. The couple, surrounded by family and friends, recite vows that focus on their commitment to each other, their dedication to the path of enlightenment, and their role in supporting and uplifting one another throughout their lives.

Another important ritual is the offering of the Five Elements. In this symbolic act, the couple offers small amounts of water, flowers, incense, light, and food to a shrine or altar. Each element represents a different aspect of life and spirituality: water symbolizes purity and clarity, flowers represent beauty and impermanence, incense signifies the aspiration for harmony, light symbolizes wisdom, and food represents nourishment and sustenance. Through this offering, the couple seeks blessings for their union and the well-being of their loved ones.

Buddhist weddings also incorporate the lighting of a unity candle. The candle represents the merging of two souls into one, symbolizing the couple's union and the illumination of their path together. The flame represents the light of wisdom and compassion that they will carry forward in their married life.

Throughout the ceremony, various Buddhist chants and mantras are recited, creating an atmosphere of sacredness and invoking blessings from the spiritual realm. These chants, often performed by monks or other ordained individuals, serve to purify and sanctify the space, inviting positive energies and divine blessings into the union.

In addition to these rituals, Buddhist weddings often incorporate traditional attire, auspicious colors, and cultural customs specific to the region or community. These elements add depth and uniqueness to each ceremony, showcasing the diverse expressions of Buddhism across different cultures.

For anthropologists studying traditional Hindu wedding ceremonies, indigenous wedding ceremonies, or any other niche within the realm of wedding rituals, exploring Buddhist weddings can provide valuable insights into the intersection of religion, culture, and marriage. By understanding the rituals and symbolism in Buddhist weddings, researchers can gain a deeper appreciation for the diverse ways in which love and commitment are celebrated across different communities and traditions.

Chapter 5: Same-Sex Marriage Ceremonies

Evolution of Same-Sex Marriage

In recent years, the concept of same-sex marriage has become a topic of great interest and discussion in various cultures and societies around the world. This subchapter aims to explore the evolution of same-sex marriage within the context of traditional Hindu wedding ceremonies and shed light on the broader implications for other indigenous, Buddhist, and interfaith wedding ceremonies.

Same-sex marriage ceremonies, although not traditionally a part of Hindu wedding rituals, have gradually found their place through the process of cultural evolution and adaptation. Anthropologists have observed how societies and cultures constantly evolve to reflect the changing beliefs, values, and attitudes of their members. This is particularly evident in the case of same-sex marriage within traditional Hindu wedding ceremonies.

Historically, Hindu wedding ceremonies were rooted in the union between a man and a woman, symbolizing the complementary nature of masculine and feminine energies. However, as societies have become more inclusive and accepting of diverse sexual orientations, the concept of same-sex marriage has gained recognition and acceptance within the Hindu community.

Anthropologists studying same-sex marriage in Hindu wedding ceremonies have noted that the evolution of this practice has been influenced by factors such as legal developments, changing social norms, and increased awareness of LGBTQ+ rights. These factors have contributed to the gradual acceptance and integration of same-sex couples into the traditional Hindu wedding rituals.

Furthermore, the evolution of same-sex marriage within Hindu wedding ceremonies has had broader implications for other indigenous, Buddhist, and interfaith wedding ceremonies. As societies become more open-minded and progressive, similar adaptations are being observed in these ceremonies as well. Same-sex couples are now participating in rituals that were once exclusively reserved for heterosexual couples, thereby challenging and reshaping long-standing traditions.

The evolution of same-sex marriage in traditional Hindu wedding ceremonies has also paved the way for destination wedding ceremonies, interfaith wedding ceremonies, and eco-friendly wedding ceremonies to embrace and celebrate love in all its forms. These ceremonies now provide a platform for same-sex couples to express their commitment and be recognized within their respective cultural and religious contexts.

In conclusion, the evolution of same-sex marriage within traditional Hindu wedding ceremonies signifies a broader societal shift towards inclusivity and acceptance. Anthropologists studying traditional Hindu wedding ceremonies, as well as indigenous, Buddhist, interfaith, and other wedding ceremonies, play a crucial role in documenting and understanding these transformations. By exploring and analyzing the evolution of same-sex marriage, anthropologists contribute to the broader discourse on love, marriage, and human rights within diverse cultural contexts.

Cultural Variations in Same-Sex Wedding Ceremonies

The concept of same-sex marriage has gained significant attention and acceptance in recent years, challenging traditional notions of matrimony across cultures. In this subchapter, we delve into the intriguing realm of cultural variations in same-sex wedding ceremonies, examining how different cultures and belief systems approach and celebrate these unions. By exploring the diverse customs and rituals associated with same-sex weddings, we aim to shed light on the intersection of culture, identity, and love.

Traditional Hindu Wedding Ceremonies: Hinduism, with its rich tapestry of rituals and traditions, has a long history of celebrating love and unity. We explore how Hindu same-sex couples navigate the complexities of their religious and cultural heritage, adapting ancient customs to reflect their unique unions.

Indigenous Wedding Ceremonies: Indigenous communities around the world have their own distinct wedding rituals, often rooted in sacred connections to the land and ancestral spirits. We examine how these communities embrace same-sex unions, honoring their cultural heritage while challenging Western notions of marriage.

Buddhist Wedding Ceremonies: Buddhism, with its emphasis on compassion and understanding, offers a unique perspective on same-sex marriage. We delve into the diverse Buddhist practices and beliefs surrounding same-sex unions, highlighting the acceptance and inclusivity found within these ceremonies.

Same-Sex Marriage Ceremonies: Beyond specific cultural contexts, we explore the broad spectrum of same-sex wedding ceremonies worldwide. From contemporary Western traditions to innovative expressions of love, we examine the creative ways in which couples celebrate their unions across different cultures.

Destination Wedding Ceremonies: With the rise of destination weddings, same-sex couples are increasingly choosing exotic locations to exchange their vows. We explore the cultural nuances and challenges faced by couples as they navigate foreign lands while honoring their own cultural identities.

Interfaith Wedding Ceremonies: When individuals from different religious backgrounds come together in love, interfaith wedding ceremonies offer a unique opportunity for cultural exchange and understanding. We explore how same-sex couples navigate the complexities of blending diverse traditions and beliefs in their unions.

African Wedding Ceremonies: Africa's rich cultural tapestry encompasses a multitude of diverse wedding rituals. We delve into the unique customs and traditions surrounding same-sex marriages in different African cultures, highlighting the resilience and celebration of love in the face of adversity.

Native American Wedding Ceremonies: Native American wedding ceremonies are deeply rooted in spirituality and community. We explore the acceptance and celebration of same-sex unions within Native American cultures, highlighting the profound connection between love, identity, and tradition.

Medieval Wedding Ceremonies: Taking a historical perspective, we examine how same-sex unions were perceived and celebrated in medieval times. By delving into ancient texts and records, we gain insight into the cultural variations and societal attitudes towards same-sex marriages in the past.

Eco-friendly Wedding Ceremonies: As the world becomes more environmentally conscious, eco-friendly wedding ceremonies are gaining popularity. We explore how same-sex couples incorporate sustainability and ethical practices into their wedding ceremonies, reflecting their commitment to both love and the planet.

In this subchapter, we embark on a fascinating journey through the diverse and intricate world of same-sex wedding ceremonies. By exploring the cultural variations and traditions surrounding these unions, we aim to deepen our understanding of the complex interplay between culture, love, and identity.

Chapter 6: Destination Wedding Ceremonies

Rise in Popularity of Destination Weddings

In recent years, there has been a significant rise in the popularity of destination weddings across various cultural and religious backgrounds. This trend has caught the attention of anthropologists, who are keen to explore its impact on traditional wedding ceremonies, including those of the Hindu, Buddhist, and indigenous communities.

Destination weddings, a concept where couples choose to tie the knot in a location away from their hometowns, have become a symbol of adventure, romance, and personalization. What was once considered a luxury reserved for the elite has now become an accessible choice for couples from diverse backgrounds.

For traditional Hindu wedding ceremonies, the rise of destination weddings has brought both advantages and challenges. On one hand, it allows couples to explore unique locations that resonate with their cultural and spiritual beliefs. For instance, some couples opt for a beachside ceremony in Bali, Indonesia, to symbolize the sacredness of water in Hindu traditions. Such choices enable couples to infuse their weddings with personal meaning and create unforgettable memories.

On the other hand, destination weddings also pose challenges to preserving the intricate rituals and customs that define Hindu wedding ceremonies. Anthropologists studying traditional Hindu weddings are intrigued by how couples navigate the need for authenticity while adapting to the constraints of a foreign location. They question whether destination weddings risk diluting the essence of the ceremony or if they offer an opportunity for cultural exchange and adaptation.

For indigenous communities and Buddhist wedding ceremonies, the rise in popularity of destination weddings signifies a potential threat to cultural heritage. Anthropologists fear that the commercialization and commodification of these ceremonies in foreign locales may lead to cultural appropriation or misrepresentation. It raises questions about the responsibility of couples and wedding planners to engage respectfully with indigenous traditions and ensure the ceremonies are conducted with cultural sensitivity.

Destination weddings have also witnessed a surge in same-sex marriage ceremonies and interfaith unions. These weddings often celebrate love and inclusivity in destinations that are more accepting and supportive of diverse relationships. Anthropologists studying these ceremonies are intrigued by the negotiation of cultural and religious boundaries within the context of destination weddings, and how they contribute to the ongoing discussions around equality and inclusion.

While destination weddings offer couples the chance to celebrate their love in extraordinary locations, they also raise concerns about their environmental impact. Eco-friendly wedding ceremonies have emerged as a niche within the destination wedding industry, focusing on sustainable practices and minimizing carbon footprints. Anthropologists studying these ceremonies explore the ways in which couples and wedding planners navigate the tension between celebrating love and protecting the environment.

In conclusion, the rise in popularity of destination weddings has sparked interest among anthropologists specializing in various wedding traditions. They investigate the impact of these weddings on cultural heritage, explore the negotiation of cultural boundaries, and examine the potential for environmental sustainability. By studying destination weddings through an anthropological lens, we can gain insights into the changing dynamics of traditional wedding ceremonies across different cultures and communities.

Cultural Adaptations in Destination Wedding Ceremonies

In recent years, destination weddings have gained immense popularity as couples seek unique and memorable experiences to celebrate their love. These weddings not only offer a picturesque backdrop but also provide an opportunity for cultural adaptations to take place, creating a fusion of traditions that reflect the diversity and richness of the global community. This subchapter explores the cultural adaptations observed in destination wedding ceremonies, focusing on the context of Traditional Hindu Wedding Ceremonies, Indigenous Wedding Ceremonies, Buddhist Wedding Ceremonies, Same-Sex Marriage Ceremonies, Interfaith Wedding Ceremonies, African Wedding Ceremonies, Native American Wedding Ceremonies, Medieval Wedding Ceremonies, and Eco-friendly Wedding Ceremonies.

Destination weddings provide a platform for couples to incorporate elements from their own cultural backgrounds, as well as the local culture of the chosen destination. For example, in Traditional Hindu Wedding Ceremonies, couples may choose to exchange vows according to ancient rituals while incorporating local customs such as wearing traditional attire or incorporating local flowers and decorations. Similarly, Indigenous Wedding Ceremonies often include traditional dances, music, and rituals specific to the indigenous community, bridging the gap between ancestral traditions and contemporary practices.

Buddhist Wedding Ceremonies also embrace cultural adaptations in destination settings. Couples may choose to have a Buddhist monk officiate the ceremony, incorporating mantras and meditation practices. Same-Sex Marriage Ceremonies, which have gained legal recognition in many countries, allow LGBTQ+ couples to adapt traditional wedding rituals to fit their own unique identities and experiences.

Interfaith Wedding Ceremonies offer an opportunity for couples from different religious backgrounds to come together and celebrate their love while honoring their respective traditions. Destination weddings provide a neutral ground where couples can blend rituals and customs from both faiths, creating a harmonious and inclusive ceremony.

African Wedding Ceremonies reflect the diversity of the continent, with couples incorporating traditional attire, music, and dance into their destination weddings. Native American Wedding Ceremonies often include sacred rituals, such as smudging or a unity pipe ceremony, to honor ancestral traditions and connect with the land.

In the context of Medieval Wedding Ceremonies, destination weddings provide a unique opportunity for couples to recreate the ambiance of a bygone era. From period costumes to medieval-inspired feasts, these ceremonies transport participants back in time, allowing them to experience the grandeur and romance of a different age.

Finally, Eco-friendly Wedding Ceremonies highlight the importance of sustainability and environmental consciousness. Couples may choose to have a destination wedding in a natural setting, such as a forest or beach, and incorporate eco-friendly practices such as using biodegradable materials or supporting local conservation efforts.

In conclusion, destination wedding ceremonies offer a platform for cultural adaptations to take place, creating a beautiful blend of traditions from different backgrounds. Whether it's incorporating elements from Traditional Hindu, Indigenous, Buddhist, African, or Native American ceremonies, or adapting rituals to fit interfaith, same-sex, medieval, or eco-friendly contexts, destination weddings allow couples to celebrate their love in a way that honors their heritage while embracing the uniqueness of the chosen destination. These adaptations not only create unforgettable experiences for the couple and their guests but also contribute to the preservation and appreciation of diverse cultural practices.

Chapter 7: Interfaith Wedding Ceremonies

Challenges and Opportunities in Interfaith Marriages

In the diverse landscape of modern society, interfaith marriages have become increasingly common. These unions, which bring together individuals from different religious backgrounds, present both unique challenges and opportunities for the couples involved. As anthropologists studying wedding ceremonies, we have the privilege of exploring the intricacies of interfaith marriages within the context of traditional Hindu wedding ceremonies, indigenous wedding ceremonies, Buddhist wedding ceremonies, same-sex marriage ceremonies, destination wedding ceremonies, African wedding ceremonies, Native American wedding ceremonies, medieval wedding ceremonies, eco-friendly wedding ceremonies, and beyond.

Interfaith marriages can be seen as a microcosm of the broader challenges and opportunities that arise when different cultures and belief systems intersect. One of the primary challenges faced by interfaith couples is the negotiation of religious practices and rituals within the context of their wedding ceremony. This negotiation often involves a delicate balance between honoring and incorporating the traditions of both partners.

For example, in a traditional Hindu wedding ceremony, the couple may face challenges in integrating elements from their respective religious backgrounds. However, this process can also be an opportunity for cultural exchange and understanding. By embracing diversity, these couples pave the way for new and innovative wedding rituals that blend traditions, creating a unique and meaningful experience for both themselves and their guests.

Furthermore, interfaith marriages offer an opportunity to challenge and transcend societal norms and expectations. Same-sex interfaith marriages, for instance, not only defy traditional gender roles but also challenge the heteronormative foundations of many religious institutions. By celebrating love and commitment across boundaries, these unions contribute to the broader movement towards inclusivity and equality.

Interfaith marriages also have the potential to foster intercultural dialogue and understanding. As anthropologists, we recognize the immense potential for learning and growth that comes from the exchange of ideas and practices. By bringing together individuals from different cultural backgrounds, these unions create opportunities for communities to bridge gaps, dispel stereotypes, and foster empathy.

In conclusion, interfaith marriages within the context of traditional Hindu wedding ceremonies, indigenous wedding ceremonies, Buddhist wedding ceremonies, same-sex marriage ceremonies, destination wedding ceremonies, African wedding ceremonies, Native American wedding ceremonies, medieval wedding ceremonies, eco-friendly wedding ceremonies, and beyond, present both challenges and opportunities. By navigating the complexities of blending different belief systems, these couples redefine wedding rituals and challenge societal norms. Moreover, they foster intercultural dialogue and understanding, contributing to a more inclusive and diverse society. As anthropologists, it is our duty to explore and celebrate the multifaceted nature of interfaith marriages, as they provide invaluable insights into the dynamics of cultural exchange and the resilience of love.

Blending Traditions in Interfaith Wedding Ceremonies

In today's multicultural and interconnected world, interfaith marriages have become increasingly common. These unions not only bring together two individuals but also two different sets of beliefs, values, and traditions. The blending of diverse cultural backgrounds offers a unique opportunity to create a wedding ceremony that celebrates the richness of each tradition while forging a new path forward. In this subchapter, we will explore the intricate tapestry of interfaith wedding ceremonies, focusing on the fusion of Hindu traditions with various other cultural and religious practices.

Traditional Hindu Wedding Ceremonies form the foundation of our exploration. By understanding the rituals, symbolism, and significance embedded in these ceremonies, we can appreciate how different elements can be seamlessly integrated into interfaith weddings. From the sacred fire in the Vedic rituals to the auspicious blessings exchanged between the couple, these ceremonies provide a strong framework for interfaith couples to build upon.

We then delve into Indigenous, Buddhist, and Native American Wedding Ceremonies, exploring how these traditions can harmoniously coexist with Hindu rituals. By highlighting the shared values of love, commitment, and spiritual connection, interfaith couples can create a new tapestry where the threads of these diverse practices are intricately woven together.

The exploration continues with Same-Sex Marriage Ceremonies, a topic that challenges traditional notions of marriage. We examine how interfaith couples navigate the complexities of blending their beliefs while also advocating for inclusivity and acceptance within their respective faith communities.

Destination Wedding Ceremonies offer a unique opportunity to infuse local customs and traditions into the interfaith wedding narrative. We explore how couples can incorporate the flavor of the destination, embracing its cultural heritage and creating a memorable experience for themselves and their guests.

We then delve into African and Medieval Wedding Ceremonies, showcasing the vibrant tapestry of rituals and customs that can be blended with Hindu traditions. From the energetic dances and drumming of African ceremonies to the grandeur and symbolism of medieval rituals, interfaith couples can draw inspiration from these diverse cultural practices.

Finally, we explore the concept of Eco-friendly Wedding Ceremonies, aligning the values of sustainability and conservation with the sacredness of the union. By incorporating eco-conscious practices into their interfaith wedding ceremonies, couples can honor their commitment to the environment and set an example for future generations.

In conclusion, the blending of traditions in interfaith wedding ceremonies is an art that requires sensitivity, creativity, and a deep understanding of the cultural and religious roots involved. By embracing the diversity of our world, interfaith couples can create a unique and meaningful celebration that honors their shared values, while also paying homage to the traditions that shaped them. Through this exploration, we hope to inspire anthropologists and individuals from various niches to embark on a journey of discovery, appreciation, and celebration of interfaith unions.

Chapter 8: Medieval Wedding Ceremonies

Historical Context of Medieval Weddings

In order to fully appreciate and understand the traditional Hindu wedding ceremonies, it is important to explore their historical context. This subchapter delves into the fascinating world of medieval weddings, shedding light on the customs and traditions that have shaped these ceremonies over the centuries.

During the medieval period, weddings were not just a union between two individuals, but a significant event that had far-reaching implications for the entire community. The rituals and practices associated with weddings were deeply ingrained in the social fabric of the time, reflecting the values, beliefs, and power dynamics of medieval society.

One of the key aspects of medieval weddings was the emphasis on religious and spiritual significance. Hinduism, Buddhism, and other indigenous belief systems played a vital role in shaping these ceremonies. The rituals were often led by religious leaders, such as priests or spiritual elders, who were responsible for conducting the sacred rites and invoking blessings for the couple.

Medieval weddings were also marked by elaborate and ornate decorations, reflecting the opulence and grandeur of the time. The use of vibrant colors, intricate designs, and luxurious fabrics added a sense of beauty and splendor to the ceremonies. These decorations not only created an enchanting ambiance but also symbolized prosperity and abundance.

Furthermore, medieval weddings were deeply rooted in cultural and regional traditions. Different regions had their own unique customs and practices, which were passed down from generation to generation. These traditions not only celebrated the union of two individuals but also reinforced social norms, values, and expectations within the community.

As anthropologists, it is essential to study medieval weddings within the wider context of wedding rituals and ceremonies. By exploring the historical context of these ceremonies, we can gain valuable insights into the cultural and social dynamics of the time. This knowledge can then be applied to our understanding of other wedding ceremonies, such as indigenous, Buddhist, and Native American weddings, as well as contemporary ceremonies like same-sex and destination weddings.

In conclusion, the historical context of medieval weddings provides a rich tapestry of customs, rituals, and traditions that have shaped traditional Hindu wedding ceremonies. By examining the religious, cultural, and regional aspects of these ceremonies, anthropologists can gain a deeper understanding of the social dynamics and significance of weddings across different cultures and time periods.

Rituals and Customs in Medieval Wedding Ceremonies

In the fascinating subchapter on "Rituals and Customs in Medieval Wedding Ceremonies," we delve into the intricate and captivating world of matrimonial traditions during the medieval era. This exploration takes us back to a time when love was intertwined with religion, social structure, and the magic of ancient customs. Through an anthropological lens, we unravel the intricacies of traditional Hindu, Buddhist, African, Native American, and other indigenous wedding ceremonies during this period.

The medieval period witnessed a rich tapestry of wedding rituals and customs across cultures, each reflecting the unique beliefs and values of the time. From the opulent Hindu weddings with their sacred fire rituals and colorful attire to the serene Buddhist ceremonies emphasizing mindfulness and meditation, we uncover the diverse ways in which love was consecrated and celebrated.

As we delve deeper, we discover the significance of the bride's attire, the symbolism of the wedding feast, and the role of family and community in medieval wedding ceremonies. We explore the interfaith wedding ceremonies that emerged during this time, as different cultures and religions came into contact and exchanged customs and traditions.

Additionally, we shine a spotlight on same-sex marriage ceremonies during the medieval period, revealing the existence of alternative narratives and celebrations that challenged societal norms. These ceremonies were often clandestine, held in secret to avoid persecution, but they serve as a testament to the resilience and strength of love.

Furthermore, we examine the concept of destination wedding ceremonies during this era, tracing the roots of modern-day desire for picturesque locations and unique experiences. We explore how couples in medieval times sought out exotic locales for their nuptials, often incorporating local customs and traditions to create unforgettable moments.

Finally, we address the importance of eco-friendly wedding ceremonies even during the medieval period. We uncover how these weddings embraced sustainability and harmony with nature, highlighting the age-old wisdom and respect for the environment that guided these ceremonies.

Through careful research and analysis, "Rituals and Customs in Medieval Wedding Ceremonies" sheds light on the diverse cultural practices and beliefs surrounding matrimony during this enthralling period. Whether you are an anthropologist or simply intrigued by the rich tapestry of human traditions, this subchapter offers a captivating and informative journey into the world of medieval wedding ceremonies.

Chapter 9: Eco-friendly Wedding Ceremonies

Importance of Sustainability in Weddings

In recent years, the concept of sustainability has gained momentum and recognition across various aspects of our lives. From food production to transportation, individuals and communities are embracing eco-friendly practices to minimize their impact on the environment. It is no surprise, then, that this movement has also made its way into the realm of weddings. Sustainability in weddings is a growing trend, and its importance cannot be overlooked, particularly when it comes to traditional Hindu, indigenous, Buddhist, same-sex, destination, interfaith, African, Native American, medieval, and eco-friendly wedding ceremonies.

Weddings are joyous celebrations that bring people together, but they can also generate a significant amount of waste and contribute to environmental degradation. However, by incorporating sustainable practices into these ceremonies, couples can minimize their carbon footprint and create a positive impact on the planet. Traditional Hindu wedding ceremonies, for example, are known for their opulence and elaborate rituals. By adopting sustainable practices such as using organic materials, reducing food waste, and opting for ethically sourced clothing and jewelry, couples can maintain the sanctity of the ceremony while also aligning it with eco-friendly principles.

Indigenous wedding ceremonies, rooted in deep connections with nature and the environment, naturally lend themselves to sustainability. By incorporating traditional practices that honor the land and its resources, couples can celebrate their love while also paying homage to their heritage. Similarly, Buddhist wedding ceremonies, with their emphasis on mindfulness and compassion, can incorporate sustainable elements that promote a harmonious relationship with the environment.

Same-sex marriage ceremonies, destination weddings, and interfaith wedding ceremonies can all benefit from embracing sustainability. These types of weddings often attract a broad audience and garner attention from diverse communities. By showcasing eco-friendly practices, couples can inspire others to follow suit and make conscious choices that reduce waste and promote a healthier planet.

Furthermore, African, Native American, and medieval wedding ceremonies, while deeply rooted in tradition, can still incorporate sustainable practices. By reimagining rituals and incorporating eco-friendly elements, couples can create a wedding experience that is both meaningful and environmentally responsible.

Lastly, eco-friendly wedding ceremonies, regardless of cultural or religious affiliation, prioritize sustainability as their core principle. From utilizing renewable energy sources to choosing locally sourced and organic food, these ceremonies set an example for others to follow.

In conclusion, the importance of sustainability in weddings cannot be understated. By incorporating eco-friendly practices into traditional Hindu, indigenous, Buddhist, same-sex, destination, interfaith, African, Native American, medieval, and eco-friendly wedding ceremonies, couples can create a positive impact on the environment while celebrating their love. These weddings have the potential to inspire others and contribute to a more sustainable future for all. As anthropologists, it is crucial that we recognize and promote the significance of sustainability in wedding ceremonies, as it reflects the evolving values and aspirations of diverse communities worldwide.

Incorporating Eco-friendly Practices in Wedding Ceremonies

As anthropologists, we are constantly exploring the rich tapestry of cultural traditions and practices that define various wedding ceremonies. In the ever-evolving world we live in, it is essential to address the pressing issue of environmental sustainability and find ways to incorporate eco-friendly practices into these sacred rituals. In this subchapter, we delve into the realm of eco-friendly wedding ceremonies, focusing on the traditional Hindu wedding ceremonies and drawing connections with other indigenous, Buddhist, same-sex, interfaith, African, Native American, and even medieval wedding ceremonies.

Wedding ceremonies are deeply rooted in cultural and religious beliefs, but they also have a significant impact on the environment. From excessive waste generation to carbon emissions, the ecological footprint of these ceremonies can be substantial. However, by embracing eco-friendly practices, we can create a more sustainable and environmentally conscious approach to these sacred unions.

One of the key aspects of eco-friendly wedding ceremonies is the incorporation of sustainable materials. Traditional Hindu ceremonies, for example, often involve the use of flowers, which can be replaced with locally sourced, seasonal blooms. By opting for organic, pesticide-free flowers, we not only support local farmers but also reduce the ecological impact of flower cultivation.

In addition to sustainable materials, energy conservation is another crucial aspect. Incorporating renewable energy sources, such as solar power, can significantly reduce the carbon footprint of wedding ceremonies. Similarly, by choosing eco-friendly transportation options and encouraging guests to carpool, we can minimize emissions associated with travel.

Food plays a central role in wedding ceremonies, and opting for locally sourced, organic, and vegetarian or vegan menus can have a profound impact on the environment. By supporting local farmers and reducing the demand for meat, we can help mitigate deforestation, water pollution, and greenhouse gas emissions associated with animal agriculture.

Furthermore, waste management is a critical consideration. Encouraging the use of reusable or biodegradable materials, such as bamboo or palm leaf plates, and implementing effective recycling and composting systems can greatly reduce the amount of waste generated during these ceremonies.

By incorporating eco-friendly practices into wedding ceremonies, we not only celebrate love and cultural traditions but also contribute to a sustainable future. By exploring the traditional Hindu wedding ceremonies through an anthropological lens, we can draw parallels with other indigenous, Buddhist, same-sex, interfaith, African, Native American, and medieval wedding ceremonies to foster a global movement towards eco-consciousness. Let us embrace the power of these sacred ties to forge a path towards a more environmentally sustainable world.

Chapter 10: Conclusion

Key Findings and Insights from Anthropological Lens

In the book "Sacred Ties: Exploring Traditional Hindu Wedding Ceremonies through Anthropological Lens," we embark on a fascinating journey to unravel the intricacies of various wedding ceremonies from around the world. Through an anthropological lens, we gain unique insights into the cultural, social, and symbolic significance of these ceremonies.

The exploration of Traditional Hindu Wedding Ceremonies offers a deep dive into the rich tapestry of Hindu culture. We uncover the elaborate rituals, the role of families, and the importance of tradition in preserving cultural heritage. From the sacred fire of the Agni Puja to the exchange of garlands during the Jaimala ceremony, we witness the profound symbolism embedded in each ritual.

Moving beyond traditional Hindu weddings, we delve into Indigenous Wedding Ceremonies, where we encounter a mosaic of diverse practices that celebrate ancestral customs and values. These ceremonies highlight the deep connection between indigenous communities and their environment, emphasizing the importance of land, spirituality, and collective identity.

Buddhist Wedding Ceremonies provide a unique perspective on the intertwining of spiritual beliefs and marital union. We explore the concept of mindfulness and compassion, which form the foundation of these ceremonies. From the recitation of sutras to the offering of prayers, we witness the harmonious blending of Buddhist philosophy and the celebration of love.

The inclusion of Same-Sex Marriage Ceremonies challenges traditional notions of marriage and explores the fluidity of love and commitment.

Through an anthropological lens, we examine the struggles and triumphs of same-sex couples in their quest for recognition and acceptance. These ceremonies serve as a powerful testament to the resilience of love, regardless of gender identities.

Destination Wedding Ceremonies offer a glimpse into the modernization and globalization of marital practices. We explore the allure of exotic locations and the commodification of weddings in the age of travel and social media. This subchapter sheds light on the cultural exchanges and tensions that arise in the context of destination weddings.

Interfaith Wedding Ceremonies provide a fascinating study of the merging of religious traditions and the negotiation of cultural identities. We explore the challenges and opportunities that arise when individuals from different faiths choose to unite in marriage. These ceremonies offer a glimpse into the potential for harmony and understanding in a multicultural world.

From African Wedding Ceremonies to Native American Wedding Ceremonies, we unveil the diversity and vibrancy of wedding customs across continents. These ceremonies highlight the importance of community, kinship, and storytelling in preserving cultural heritage. We witness the power of music, dance, and attire in conveying ancestral wisdom and celebrating love.

Even Medieval Wedding Ceremonies, though seemingly distant in time, offer valuable insights into the historical and social dynamics of marital practices. We unravel the symbolism behind medieval rituals, the role of church and state, and the significance of dowries and contracts. These ceremonies serve as a reminder of the cultural and societal transformations that have shaped our modern understanding of marriage.

Lastly, Eco-friendly Wedding Ceremonies shed light on the emerging trend of environmentally conscious weddings. We explore the incorporation of sustainable practices, from organic food to eco-friendly decorations. These ceremonies demonstrate the potential for celebrating love while minimizing our ecological footprint.

In conclusion, "Sacred Ties: Exploring Traditional Hindu Wedding Ceremonies through Anthropological Lens" offers anthropologists a comprehensive and enlightening journey through various wedding ceremonies. From traditional to modern, from ancient to contemporary, this book provides a deep understanding of the cultural, social, and symbolic dimensions of weddings, appealing to a wide range of niches within the anthropological field.

Implications for Future Research and Understanding Traditional Wedding Ceremonies

As anthropologists delve deeper into the study of traditional wedding ceremonies, new insights and understandings emerge, shedding light on the diverse cultural practices and beliefs surrounding these sacred rituals. This subchapter aims to explore the implications for future research and the significance of understanding traditional wedding ceremonies from an anthropological lens, with a particular focus on Hindu, indigenous, Buddhist, same-sex, destination, interfaith, African, Native American, medieval, and eco-friendly wedding ceremonies.

Traditional Hindu wedding ceremonies encompass a wide range of rituals, each carrying its unique symbolism and cultural significance. By studying these ceremonies, anthropologists can gain a deeper understanding of the complex social structures, gender roles, and familial dynamics within Hindu communities. Future research could delve into the changing dynamics of Hindu weddings in modern times, the influence of globalization on these rituals, and the ways in which they adapt to contemporary social and cultural contexts.

Indigenous wedding ceremonies provide a rich tapestry of cultural practices that reflect the deep connection between communities and their natural surroundings. Anthropologists can explore the spiritual and ecological dimensions of these ceremonies, highlighting the importance of preserving indigenous knowledge and rituals for sustainable futures. Research in this area can contribute to the revitalization of indigenous cultures and the promotion of cultural diversity.

Buddhist wedding ceremonies offer a unique insight into the intersection of religious and cultural practices. By studying these ceremonies, anthropologists can uncover the ways in which Buddhism shapes marital relationships and the role of spirituality in the union. Future research could explore the variations in Buddhist wedding rituals across different regions and the ways in which these ceremonies adapt to contemporary values.

The recognition and celebration of same-sex marriage ceremonies have gained significant attention in recent years. Anthropological research can contribute to understanding the social, cultural, and legal implications of these ceremonies, as well as the challenges faced by LGBTQ+ communities in different cultural contexts. Future studies could focus on the ways in which same-sex marriage ceremonies challenge and redefine traditional notions of marriage and family.

Destination wedding ceremonies have become increasingly popular in the modern era. Anthropologists can explore the commodification of these ceremonies, the impact on local communities, and the ways in which cultural practices are adapted to suit the desires of couples from diverse backgrounds. Future research could examine the power dynamics between tourists and local communities in destination wedding contexts.

Interfaith wedding ceremonies offer a fascinating glimpse into the blending of different religious traditions and the negotiation of cultural and religious identities within a marriage. Anthropologists can investigate the ways in which these ceremonies navigate the complexities of interfaith relationships, highlighting the role of compromise, negotiation, and adaptation.

African wedding ceremonies provide rich insights into the cultural diversity and complexity of the African continent. Anthropological research in this area can contribute to a deeper understanding of the social, political, and economic dimensions of these ceremonies, as well as the ways in which they reflect the changing dynamics of African societies.

Native American wedding ceremonies offer a unique perspective on the intersection of spirituality, tradition, and cultural identity. Anthropologists can explore the role of these ceremonies in preserving indigenous knowledge, cultural heritage, and community cohesion. Future research could investigate the impact of colonization and globalization on Native American wedding ceremonies and the ways in which these rituals adapt to contemporary realities.

Medieval wedding ceremonies offer a glimpse into the historical practices and beliefs surrounding marriage in medieval societies. By studying these ceremonies, anthropologists can gain insights into the power dynamics, gender roles, and social hierarchies prevalent during this period. Future research could explore the ways in which medieval wedding ceremonies shaped and reflected societal norms and values.

Eco-friendly wedding ceremonies have gained traction as individuals and communities strive to minimize their ecological footprints. Anthropologists can investigate the ways in which these ceremonies promote sustainable practices, cultural preservation, and community engagement. Future research could explore the challenges and opportunities faced by couples and communities in organizing eco-friendly wedding ceremonies.

In conclusion, the implications for future research and understanding traditional wedding ceremonies are vast and multifaceted. By studying these ceremonies through an anthropological lens, researchers can contribute to the preservation of cultural heritage, the promotion of cultural diversity, and the appreciation of the complexities and nuances of marriage rituals across different cultural contexts.

www.ingramcontent.com/pod-product-compliance
Lightning Source LLC
Chambersburg PA
CBHW051309160726
47994CB00003B/1385